I'm not so good at swimming yet.

But I can sure blow bubbles.

Sometimes I blow them far too big.

It gets me into trouble.

I can count to 23,

No, make that 24.

One day I'll count to 25,

It's just one number more.

I am faster than the wind.

I'm good at winning races.

I'm good at putting on my shoes.

I'm just not great with laces.

I'm very good with A, B, C.

And U,- it's time we met.

But I'm not so good with X, Y, Z,

Or reading big words yet.

I'm not too bad at giving hugs.

I'm good at giving smiles.

I'm not so good with cleaning teeth.

It's going to take a while.

I'm very good at jumping rope.

But I'm afraid to climb.

One day I'll face up to my fears.

But now is not the time.

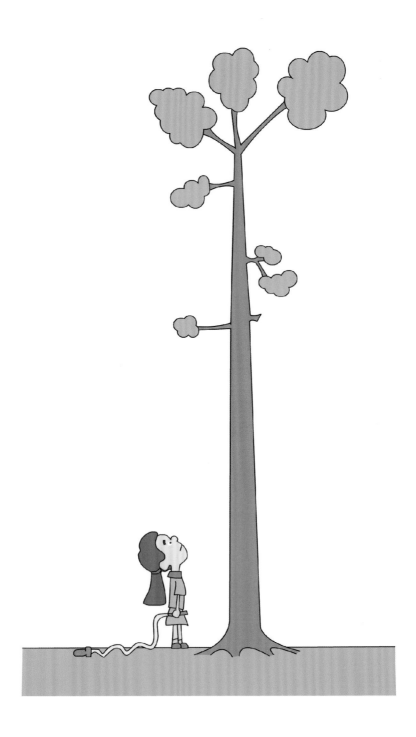

I'm very good at dressing up.
I'm great at finding gold.
I'm not so good with buttons yet.
Or doing what I'm told.

I'm not so good with this yet.
At that I'm quite the whiz.
Learning new stuff sure takes time.
That's just the way it is.

Activities

Talk about what these images are telling you about the story.

Activities

Talk about what these images are telling you about the story.

Activities

Talk about what these images are telling you about the story.

Activities

Talk about what these images are telling you about the story.